Everything Relaxed Coloring Book

Adult Coloring Book

KAILEAH NELSON

Kaileah Nelson

ISBN: 1546427759
ISBN-13: 978-1546427759

Kaileah Nelson

Rose Vine

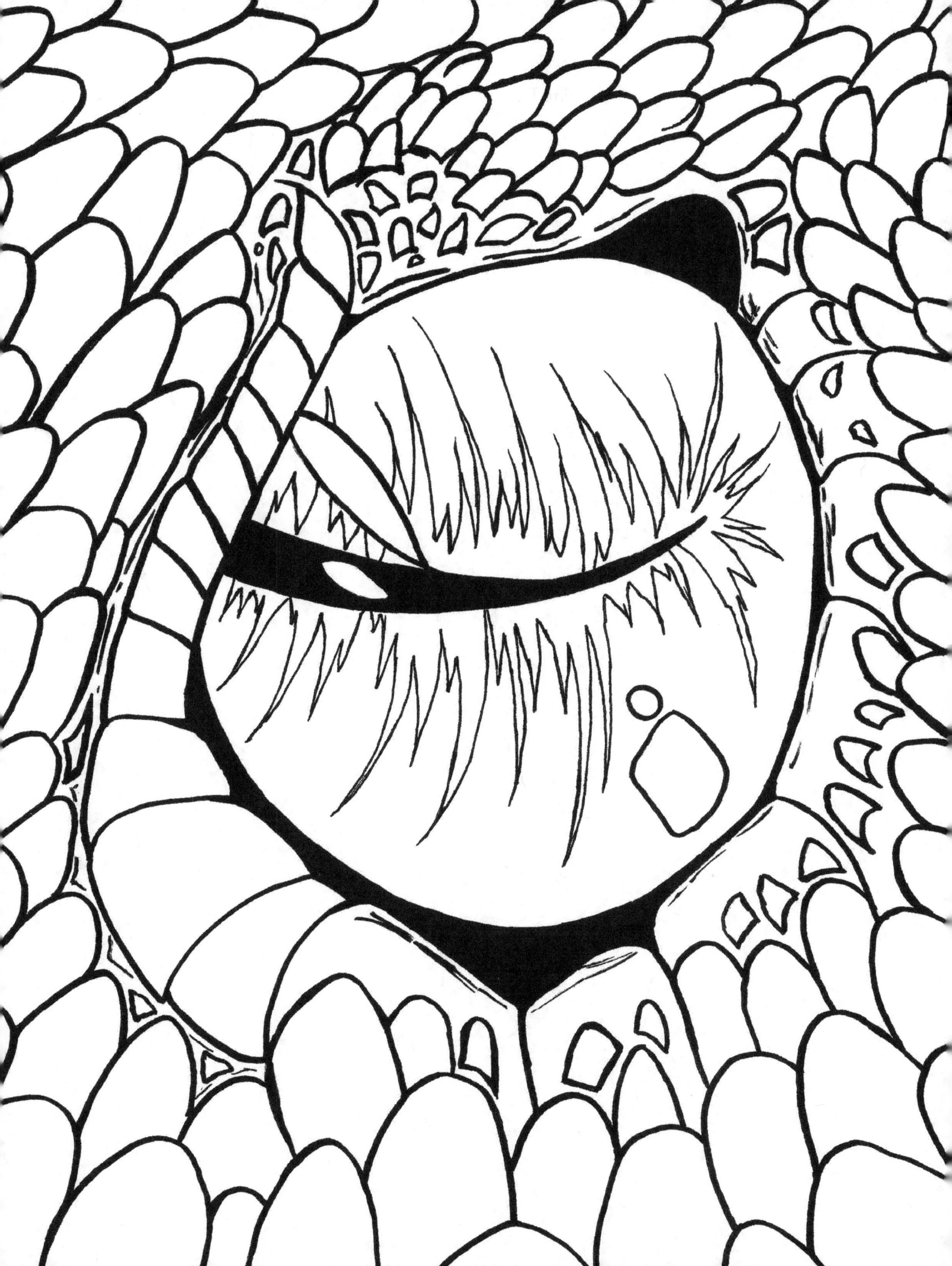

Kaileah Nelson

The Eye of the Dragon

Kaileah Nelson

Tails and Scales

Kaileah Nelson

The Hummingbird

Kaileah Nelson

Elven Morning

Kaileah Nelson

Elven Morning

Kaileah Nelson

Ocean Sunset

Kaileah Nelson

Ocean Sunset

Kaileah Nelson

Royal Family of Mers

Kaileah Nelson

Ice Caverns

Ice Caverns

Kaileah Nelson

Clockwork Kitty

Kaileah Nelson

Moon Fairies' Dance

Kaileah Nelson

Breaking Time

Kaileah Nelson

Stellar

Kaileah Nelson

Illusion

Kaileah Nelson

Enchanted Forest

Kaileah Nelson

Ruin Castle

Kaileah Nelson

Dancing Octopi

Kaileah Nelson

Galaxies

Kaileah Nelson

Crazy Sky

Kaileah Nelson

Brownies Play

Kaileah Nelson

The Hidden Library

Kaileah Nelson

Moonlit Forest

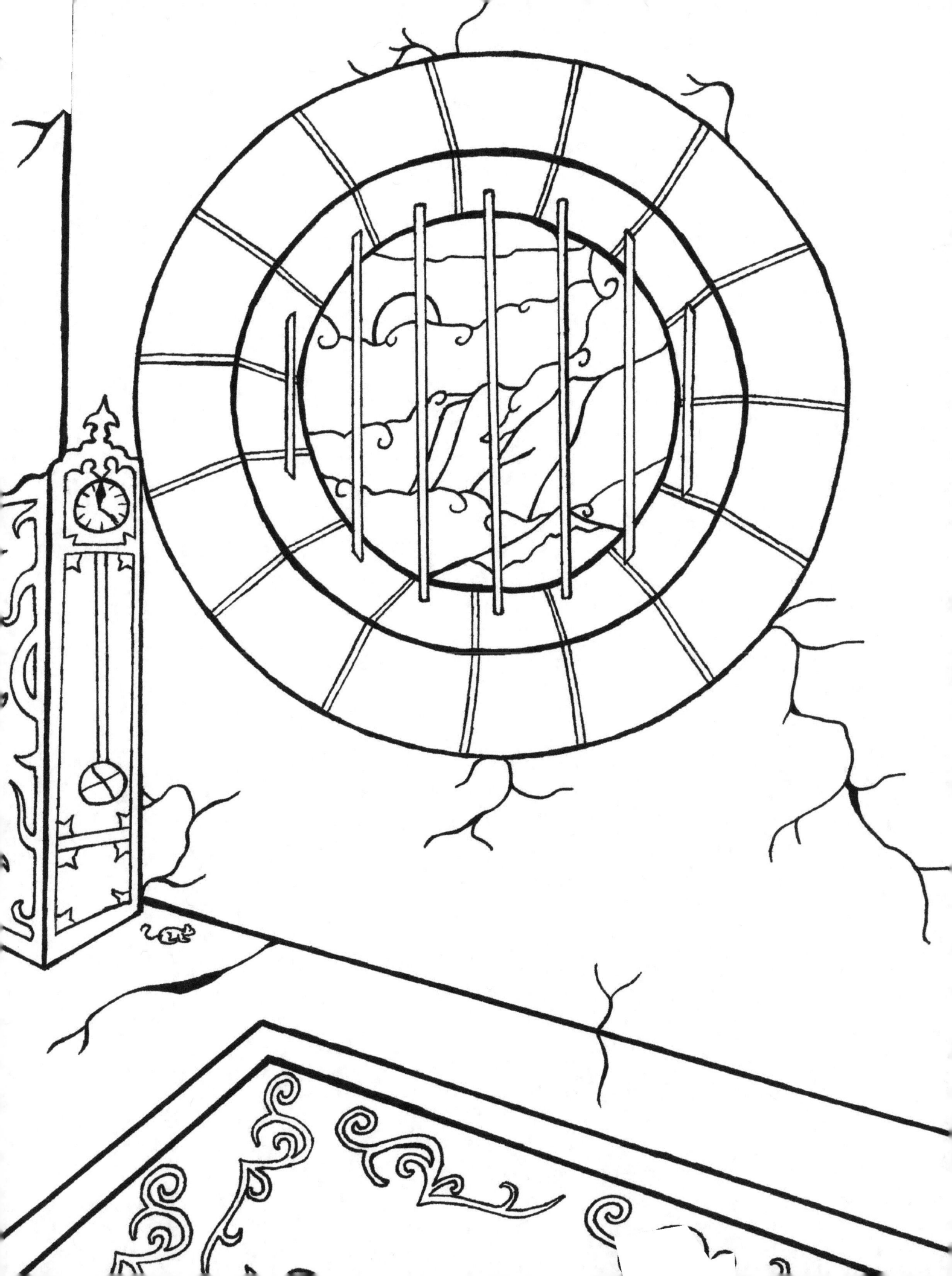

Kaileah Nelson

Sky Castle

Kaileah Nelson

Flight of the Dragonfly

Kaileah Nelson

Kaileah Nelson

The Humbunny in the Roses
-Thank you K.D. Nelson for permitting me to bring to life the Humbunny

Kaileah Nelson

The Jewel

Kaileah Nelson

The Jewel

Illustrator

Kaileah Nelson is an artist who shares the passion for creating beautiful, fun and relaxing coloring books. She knows that when you create you have an anxiety free day. Which is something she believes everyone should have.

At seventeen she has Illustrated many books, For K.D. Nelson and The Dragon Bug Sisters, and now she wants to know what you may think or a suggestion of something you wish to color. You can let her know by reaching her at, kaileah105@hotmail.com.

www.ingramcontent.com/pod-product-compliance
Lightning Source LLC
Chambersburg PA
CBHW081424280526

45788CB00009B/3219